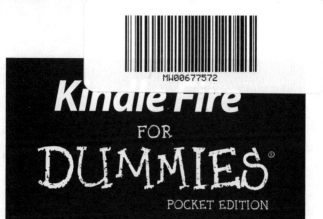

Kindle Fire

FOR

DUMMIES®

POCKET EDITION

by Nancy C. Muir

WILEY

John Wiley & Sons, Inc.

Kindle Fire™ For Dummies®

Published by
John Wiley & Sons, Inc.
111 River Street
Hoboken, NJ 07030-5774

www.wiley.com

WILEY

Table of Contents

Publisher's Acknowledgments

We're proud of this book; please send us your comments at http://dummies.custhelp.com. For other comments, please contact our Customer Care Department within the U.S. at 877-762-2974, outside the U.S. at 317-572-3993, or fax 317-572-4002.

Some of the people who helped bring this book to market include the following:

Acquisitions and Editorial

Project Editor and Editorial Manager: Jodi Jensen

Sr. Acquisitions Editor: Katie Mohr

Copy Editor: Laura K. Miller

Technical Editor: Earl Boysen

Editorial Assistant: Amanda Graham

Sr. Editorial Assistant: Cherie Case

Photographers: Michael Trent, Kevin Kirschner

Cover Photo: ©iStockphoto.com / TUNA TIRKAZ (background); image of device by Michael Trent

Composition Services

Project Coordinator: Kristie Rees

Layout and Graphics: Samantha K. Cherolis, Lavonne Roberts, Brent Savage

Proofreader: Betty Kish

Additional cover images: Angry Birds Free, Rovio Entertainment Ltd. ESPN ScoreCenter, ESPN Inc. Basic Spanish For Dummies, Skava

Publishing and Editorial for Technology Dummies

Richard Swadley, Vice President and Executive Group Publisher

Andy Cummings, Vice President and Publisher

Mary Bednarek, Executive Acquisitions Director

Mary C. Corder, Editorial Director

Publishing for Consumer Dummies

Kathleen Nebenhaus, Vice President and Executive Publisher

Composition Services

Debbie Stailey, Director of Composition Services

Introduction

● ●

*K*indle Fire is a very affordable way to get at all
kinds of media, from music and videos to books
and colorful magazines. It's also a device that allows
you to browse the Internet, check your e-mail, and
read documents. Its portability makes it incredibly
useful for people on the go in today's fast-paced world.

In this book, I introduce you to all the cool features of
Kindle Fire, providing tips and advice for getting the
most out of this ingenious little tablet. I help you find
your way around its attractive and easy-to-use interface, and even recommend some neat apps that make
your device more functional and fun.

"If Kindle Fire is so easy to use, why do I need a
book?" you may be asking yourself. When I first sat
down with Kindle Fire, it took about three or four
days of poking around to find settings, features, and
ways to buy and locate my content and apps. When
was the last time you had four days to spare? I've
spent the time so that you can quickly and easily get
the hang of all the Kindle Fire features and discover a
few tricks I bet your friends won't uncover for quite a
while.

Icons Used in This Book

Icons are little pictures in the margin of this book that
alert you to special types of advice or information,
including

These short words of advice draw your attention to faster, easier, or alternative ways of getting things done with Kindle Fire.

 When you see this icon, you'll know that I'm emphasizing important information for you to keep in mind as you use a feature.

 There aren't too many ways you can get in trouble with the Kindle Fire, but in those few situations where some action might be irreversible, I include warnings so you avoid any pitfalls.

Get Going!

Time to get that Kindle Fire out of its box, set it up, and get going with all the fun, entertaining things it makes available to you. Have fun!

Chapter 1

Overview of the Kindle Fire

· ·

In This Chapter

▶ Comparing Kindle Fire to the competition

▶ Surveying all of the Kindle Fire's features

· ·

*A*mazon, the giant online retailer, just happens to have access to more content (music, movies, audio books, and so on) than just about anybody on the planet. And now, the Kindle Fire, an awesome machine in its own right, offers the key to that treasure chest of content.

In this chapter, you get an overview of the Kindle Fire: how it compares to competing devices and its key features.

How Kindle Fire Stacks Up

Let's start at the beginning. A *tablet* is a hand-held computer with an onscreen keyboard and apps that allow you to play games, read e-books, check e-mail, browse the web, and more.

In the world of tablets, the first device to hit big was iPad, and then subsequent tablets, such as Samsung Galaxy and HP TouchPad, appeared. No tablet since iPad seems to have gained a foothold in the market up to now, so the logical comparison here is to the iPad.

Kindle Fire is lighter and smaller than iPad, sporting a 7-inch display (see Figure 1-1) and weighing only 14.6 ounces, versus iPad's 9.7-inch display and 1.3-pound frame. That smaller, lighter form factor makes the Kindle Fire easier to hold with one hand than the iPad.

Kindle Fire has a projected battery life of eight hours, versus iPad's ten hours, but those two hours are a result of a lighter-weight battery (and therefore, a lighter device), which is probably a fair trade-off for most. The screen resolution on the Kindle Fire's bright color screen is about on par with the iPad screen.

Figure 1-1: The neat size and weight of Kindle Fire make it easy to hold.

Kindle Fire has 8GB of internal storage, versus 16, 32, or 64GB on the various iPad models, but there's a reason for that. Amazon provides free storage for all your Amazon-purchased content in the *Cloud* (a huge collection of online storage) so you can stream video and music instead of downloading it, if you like.

Kindle Fire also has some very intelligent technology that allows your browser to take advantage of the Cloud to display your web pages faster.

In its first generation model, Kindle Fire has no cameras and no microphone, which means you can't take pictures or make phone calls with it.

In several ways, Kindle Fire is easy to use, with a simple Android-based touchscreen interface, and it's a great device for consuming media — and what a lot of media Amazon makes available! Kindle Fire also offers a brand new browser named Silk, an e-mail client, and the fabulous Kindle e-reader (see Figure 1-2).

Key Features of Kindle Fire

Kindle Fire is one spiffy little device with all the things most people want from a tablet packed into an easy-to-hold package: e-mail, web browsing, players for video and music content, an e-reader, a great online content store, access to tens of thousands of Android apps, and so on. In the following sections, you get to explore all these great features.

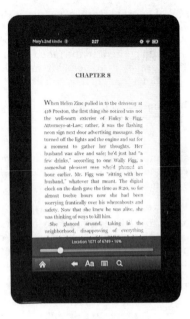

Figure 1-2: Where it all started, with Kindle e-reader functionality.

Pre-installed functionality

Here's a rundown of the functionality you get out of the box from pre-installed apps:

- ✔ E-reader to read both books and periodicals
- ✔ Music player
- ✔ Video player
- ✔ Contacts app

- ✔ Document reader for Word, PDF, RTF, and HTML format files

- ✔ Silk web browser

- ✔ Gallery in which you can view and make a very few edits to photos (rotate and crop)

- ✔ E-mail client (meaning you can set up Kindle Fire to access your existing e-mail accounts)

 There is a free version of Quickoffice that comes pre-installed on your Kindle Fire. This app offers a mini-suite of productivity products, including a word processor, spreadsheet, and presentation software.

Kindle Fire gives you the ability to

- ✔ Shop at Amazon for music, video, apps, books, and periodicals.

- ✔ Store Amazon-purchased content in the Amazon Cloud and play music and video selections from the Cloud, instead of downloading them to your device.

- ✔ Send documents to yourself at a Kindle e-mail address that's assigned when you register your device.

- ✔ *Sideload* content from your computer to your Kindle Fire by using a micro-B cable that you can purchase separately. Using this cable (see Figure 1-3), you can copy photos, music, videos, and documents (Word or PDF) from any source onto your Kindle Fire.

The magic of Whispersync

If you've ever owned a Kindle e-reader, you know that downloading content to it has always been seamless. All you need for this process is access to a Wi-Fi network. Then, you simply order a book, and within moments, it appears on your Kindle device.

Figure 1-3: The micro-B cable, sold separately for around $10.

Kindle Fire enjoys the same kind of easy download capability for books, music, video, and periodicals.

Whispersync helps sync items such as bookmarks you've placed in e-books or the last place you watched in a video across various devices. For example, say you have the Kindle e-reader app on your Kindle Fire, PC, and smartphone. Wherever you left off reading, whatever notes you entered, and whatever pages you've bookmarked will be synced among all the devices without you having to lift a finger.

Content, content, content!

Kindle Fire is meant as a device you use to consume media, meaning that you can play/read all kinds of music, movies, TV shows, podcasts, e-books, magazines, and newspapers. Amazon has built up a huge amount of content, from print and audio books (one million titles and counting in the Kindle Store) to movies and TV shows (100,000 movies and TV series), music (17 million songs), and hundreds of your favorite magazines.

You can find various kinds of content in the Amazon store by clicking the Store button in the libraries you access through the Kindle Fire Home screen. Tap Newsstand to shop for periodicals (see Figure 1-4) and Music to shop for songs and albums, tap Video to go directly to the Amazon VideoStore, and tap Apps to shop the Amazon Appstore. All the content you purchase is backed up on the Amazon Cloud.

See Chapter 4 for more about buying content and apps for your Kindle Fire.

Figure 1-4: Amazon's magazine selection is constantly growing.

You can also transfer documents from your computer or send them via e-mail and read them on Kindle Fire. Note that docs are not backed up in the Amazon Cloud.

Browsing with Amazon Silk

Silk is Amazon's new browser (see Figure 1-5). Silk is simple to use, but the real benefits of Amazon Silk are all about browsing performance.

Figure 1-5: Amazon Silk offers simple-to-use browsing tools.

Amazon Silk is touted as a "Cloud-accelerated split browser." In plain English, this means that the browser can use the power of Amazon's servers to load the pages of a website quickly. Because parts of the process of loading web pages are handled not on Kindle Fire, but on servers in the Cloud, your pages simply display faster.

In addition, you get what's called a persistent connection, which means that your tablet is always connected to the Amazon Internet backbone (the routes that data travels to move among networks online) whenever it has access to a Wi-Fi connection.

Another fascinating ability of Silk is the way it filters content to deliver it faster. Say you open a news site, such as MSN or CNN. Obviously, millions of others are accessing these pages on the same day. If most of those folks choose to open the Entertainment page after reading the home page of the site, Silk essentially predicts what page you might open next and pre-loads it. If you choose to go to that page, too, it appears instantly.

Taking advantage of free Cloud storage

Kindle Fire has less storage space (8GB) than some competing tablets. That amount of storage will probably work just fine for you, however, because when you own a Kindle Fire, you get free, unlimited Cloud storage for all digital content purchased from Amazon (not the content you copy onto Kindle Fire from your computer by using a micro-B cable). This means that books, movies, music, and apps are held online for you to stream or download at any time, instead of being stored on your Kindle Fire.

This storage means that you don't use up your Kindle Fire memory. As long as you have a Wi-Fi connection, you can stream content from Amazon's Cloud at anytime. If you'll be away from a connection, download an item (such as an episode of your favorite TV show) and watch it, and then remove it from your device the next time you're within range of a Wi-Fi network. The content is still available in the Cloud: You can download that content again or stream it anytime you like.

A world of color on the durable display

The display on Kindle Fire offers 16 million colors (see Figure 1-6). The high-resolution screen makes for very crisp colors when you're watching that hit movie or reading a colorful magazine. *In-plane switching* is a technology that gives you a wide viewing angle on the Kindle Fire screen. The result is that, if you want to share your movie with a friend sitting next to you on the couch, she'll have no problem seeing what's on the screen from that side angle.

Figure 1-6: The bright display on Kindle Fire makes media shine.

In addition, the glass screen is coated with layers that make it extra strong — 30 times harder than plastic — so it should withstand most of the bumps and scratches you throw at it.

Of course, you should avoid dropping your Kindle Fire, exposing it to extreme temperatures, or spilling liquids on it. The User Guide also advises that, if you do spill liquids, you shouldn't heat the device in your microwave to dry it off.

Note that Kindle Fire, although it has a screen that renders images crisply, is not a high-definition device. Although you can purchase and play HD versions of movies and TV shows, they'll play just like non-HD media. See Chapter 6 for more about playing video content.

Understanding the value of Amazon Prime

Kindle Fire comes with one free month of Amazon Prime. I've been an Amazon Prime member for years, so I can tell you firsthand that this service is one of the best deals out there. During your free month, Prime will allow you to get a lot of perks, such as free two-day shipping on thousands of items sold through Amazon and free instant videos.

If you decide to pick up the service after your free month, it will cost you $79 a year. So, what do you get for your money?

Prime includes free two-day shipping on millions of items and overnight shipping for only $3.99. Not every item offered on Amazon is eligible for Prime, but enough are that it's a wonderful savings in time and money over the course of a year. You can probably pay for the membership with the free shipping on the first two or three orders you place. And getting your Prime stuff in only two days every time is sweet.

In addition, Prime membership gives you access to Prime Instant Videos, which include thousands of movies and TV shows that can be streamed to your Kindle Fire absolutely free. We're not talking obscure 1970s sleepers, here: Recent additions to Prime Instant Videos include TV shows such as all the *Star Trek* series and the hit series *Frasier,* and award winning movies such as *Elizabeth* and *Notting Hill.*

 If you already have a paid Amazon Prime account, you don't get an extra month for free, sad to say. And if you don't have a Prime account, your 30 days of a free account starts from the time you activate your Kindle Fire, not the first time you make a Prime purchase or stream a Prime Instant Video. So, my suggestion is to start using it right away to take full advantage and decide whether the paid membership is for you.

Chapter 2

Kindle Fire Quickstart

* *

In This Chapter
▶ Setting up your Kindle Fire
▶ Playing with libraries, the Carousel, and Favorites
▶ Using a micro-B cable to transfer

* *

*I*n this chapter, I help you to get familiar with what comes in the box, explore the interface (what you see on the screen), and start to use your fingers to interact with the touchscreen.

Get Going with Kindle Fire

The first time you turn on Kindle Fire, you register it and link it to your Amazon account so that you can shop till you drop. Although your device probably comes with a decent battery charge, at some point you'll inevitably have to charge the battery. I cover that in the section "Charging the battery," later in this chapter.

Opening the box

Your Kindle Fire arrives in a plain brown box (see Figure 2-1). The Kindle Fire itself rests on top of a piece of hard plastic, and a small brown card with

some Kindle Fire basics printed on both sides is slot-
ted into the lid of the box. Beneath the piece of plastic
rests a charger in a paper sleeve. That's it. Remove
the protective plastic from the device, and you're
ready to get going.

Figure 2-1: The Kindle Fire packaging.

Turning the device on and off

After you get the tablet out of its packaging, it's time
to turn it on. The Kindle Fire sports a Power button

on the bottom of the device when you hold it in portrait orientation (see Figure 2-2). Next to the Power button is a port where you can insert a micro-B cable to connect the Kindle Fire to your computer, along with a headphone jack.

Headphone jack   Power button

Port for micro-B card

Figure 2-2: The Power button sits on the bottom of your Kindle Fire.

To turn the device on, press the Power button. If you're starting up for the first time, you're taken through a series of setup screens (see the following section for more about this). After you go through the setup process and register your Kindle Fire, you see the Home screen shown in Figure 2-3 on startup. The Status Bar gives you information about items such as your device's battery charge, as well as access to a Quick

Settings menu for universal Kindle Fire settings; the
Options bar at the bottom of the screen provides
access to settings and tools that are context-specific
(they vary depending on what you're doing at the time).

If you want to lock your Kindle Fire, which is akin to
putting a laptop computer to sleep, tap the Power
button again. To shut down your Kindle, press and
hold the Power button until a message appears offering you the options to Shut Down or Cancel.

Status bar

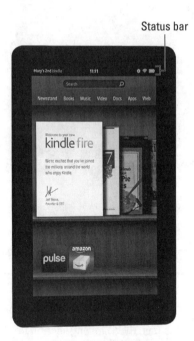

Figure 2-3: The Kindle Fire Home screen.

If your Kindle Fire becomes non-responsive, you can press and hold the Power button for 20 seconds, and it should come to life again.

Getting to know the touchscreen

Before you work through the setup screens for your Kindle Fire, it will help if you to get to know the basics of navigating the touchscreen — especially if you've never used a touchscreen before:

- ✔ Tap an item to select it or double-tap an item (such as an app) to open it.

- ✔ If your Kindle Fire goes to a lock screen after a period of inactivity, swipe your finger from right to left across the yellow band that has an arrow on one end (see Figure 2-4) to go to the Home screen.

- ✔ Double-tap to enlarge text and double-tap again to return the text to its original size. Note, this works only in certain locations, such as when displaying a web page in the Silk browser.

- ✔ Place your fingers apart on a screen and pinch them together to zoom in on the current view; place your fingers together on the screen and then move them apart (unpinch) to enlarge the view.

- ✔ Swipe left to move to the next page in apps such as the e-reader or the Silk web browser. Swipe to the right to move to the previous page.

- ✔ Swipe up and down to scroll up and down a web page.

These touchscreen gestures will help you get around most of the content and setup screens you encounter.

Arrow

11:11 Tuesday, November 15

Figure 2-4: Swipe this arrow to go to the Home screen.

Setting up your Kindle Fire

When you turn Kindle Fire on for the first time, you see a series of screens that help you set up and register the device. Don't worry: There aren't many questions, and you know all the answers.

The first screen is titled Welcome to Kindle Fire. This is the point in the setup process at which you connect to a Wi-Fi network. You need this connection to register your device.

At some point during this setup procedure you may be prompted to plug your adapter in if your battery charge is low. You may also be notified that the latest Kindle software is downloading and have to wait for that process to complete before you can move forward.

Follow these steps to register and set up your Kindle Fire:

1. **In the Connect to a Network list, tap an available network.**

    Kindle Fire connects to the network (you may need to enter a password and then tap Connect to access an available network) and then displays the Time Zone screen (see Figure 2-5).

2. **Tap to select a time zone from the list provided.**

    For countries other than the United States, tap More and choose from the provided list. Then tap the Back button in the bottom-left corner to return to the Time Zone screen.

3. **Tap Continue.**

4. **On the Register Your Kindle screen that appears (see Figure 2-6), enter your Amazon account information, e-mail address, and a password; then skip to Step 7.**

    See Step 5 if you don't have an Amazon account.

    You can choose to deselect the Show Password checkbox so that your password doesn't appear on your screen as you type it. This protects your password from prying eyes.

Figure 2-5: Choose your time zone.

5. **If you don't have an Amazon account, click the New to Amazon? Create an Account link.**

   This link takes you to the Create an Amazon Account screen, with fields for entering your name, e-mail address, and password (which you have to retype to confirm).

6. **Enter this information, and then tap Continue.**

7. **If you want to read the terms of registration, tap the By Registering, You Agree to All of the Terms Found Here link.**

8. **When you finish reading the terms, tap the Close button to return to the registration screen.**

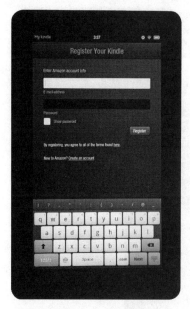

Figure 2-6: Register your Kindle Fire to use it.

9. **To complete the registration, tap the Register button.**

   A final screen appears saying Welcome to Kindle Fire: Hello *<Your Name>*. There's also a link labeled Not *<Your Name>*? If, for some reason, you aren't you (for example, you may have entered your account information incorrectly), tap the Not *<Your Name>* link to change your account information.

This is the point at which the Kindle Fire may download the latest Kindle software. Sit back, relax, and anticipate using your new toy. When the download finishes, tap the Get Started Now button, and you can

view a series of quick tips to get you started with
Kindle Fire, as shown in Figure 2-7. (If you need more
help at any time, you can refer to the User's Guide in
the Kindle Fire Docs library.) Tap Next to move
through this tour; on the last of the three screens, tap
Close to get going with Kindle Fire.

Figure 2-7: This very quick tutorial covers the basics of using
Kindle Fire.

Charging the battery

Kindle Fire has a battery life of seven-and-a-half hours
for Wi-Fi–connected activities, such as web browsing,
streaming movies, and listening to music from the
Cloud. If you're a bookworm who's more into the

printed word than media, you'll be happy to hear that you get about eight-and-a-half hours of reading downloaded books with wireless turned off.

You charge the battery with the provided charger. Attach the smaller end of the charger to your Kindle Fire's micro-B port, located near the Power button, and the other end to a wall outlet. If completely depleted, the Kindle Fire takes about four hours to charge.

 There's a battery indicator on the Status bar that runs across the top of the Kindle Fire screen so you can check to see if your battery is running low.

Getting to Know the Interface

The interface you see on the Kindle Home screen (see Figure 2-8) is made up of three areas. At the top, you see a set of buttons that take you to the Kindle Fire libraries that contain various types of content. In the middle of the screen is the Carousel. The Carousel contains images of items you recently used that you can flick with your finger to scroll through and tap to open. Finally, the bottom portion of the Home screen contains items you've saved to your Favorites (plus a few items Amazon pre-saved there for you).

Accessing Kindle Fire libraries

Kindle Fire libraries are where you access downloaded content, as well as content stored by Amazon in the Cloud. Libraries (with the exception of the Docs library) also offer a Store button that you can tap to go online to browse and buy more content.

Carousel

Library buttons

Favorites

Figure 2-8: This graphical interface is fun to move around with the flick of a finger.

Tap any library button to open a library of downloaded and archived content: Newsstand, Books, Music, Video, or Apps. Note that there's also a Docs button, where documents that you sideload from your computer or receive as e-mail attachments in your Kindle inbox are placed.

Understanding the Cloud

Everything you buy using Kindle Fire is purchased through Amazon or its affiliates on the Amazon site. That content is downloaded to your device through a technology called *Whispersync*, which requires a Wi-Fi connection.

When you purchase content, you can choose whether to keep it in the Cloud or download it to your Kindle Fire. If you download it, you can access it whether or not you're in range of a Wi-Fi network. At any time, you can remove content from the device, and it will be archived in the Cloud for you to stream to your device (music or video) or re-download (music, video, books, and magazines) whenever you like.

The Video app opens to the Amazon store, rather than a library, because in most cases, it's not very prudent to download video content to your Kindle Fire. Because this type of content takes up so much of your memory, it's preferable to play video from Amazon's Cloud (which is called *streaming*).

 There's also a Web button at the far right that you can tap to open the Silk web browser. Find out more about going online and using the browser in Chapter 4.

In a library, such as the Music library shown in Figure 2-9, you can tap the Device or Cloud tab. The Device tab shows you only content you have down-loaded; the Cloud tab displays all your purchases or free content stored in Amazon's Cloud library, including content you've downloaded to the Kindle Fire.

You can download archived content at any time or remove downloaded content to the Cloud. You can also view the contents of libraries in different ways, depending on which library you're in. For example, you can view Music library contents by categories such as Songs, Artists, and Albums.

 When you go to a library and tap the Cloud button, content that's not currently downloaded sports a little downloading arrow in the bottom-right corner. You can re-download that content by tapping the item at any time.

Figure 2-9: Your Music library provides access to all your musical content.

 It's possible to download video, which is useful if you'll be out of range of a Wi-Fi connection. But I recommend removing the content from your device when you're done watching and back in Wi-Fi range. Removing content from Kindle Fire involves pressing it with your finger and choosing Remove from Device from the menu that appears.

As mentioned before, you can also sideload content you've obtained from other sources, such as iTunes, to your Kindle Fire libraries. Sideloading involves purchasing a micro-B cable (about $10 from Amazon but also available from other sources), and then using the cable to connect Kindle Fire to your computer and copying content to Kindle Fire. See the section "Using a Micro-B Cable to Transfer Data," later in this chapter, for more about this process.

Playing with the Carousel

If you've used an Android device, such as a smartphone, you've probably encountered the Carousel concept. On Kindle Fire, items you've used recently are displayed chronologically in the Carousel (see Figure 2-10), with the most recent item you used on top. You can swipe your finger to the right or left to flick through the Carousel contents. When you find an item you want to view or play, tap to open it.

Whatever you tap opens in the associated player or reader. Music will open in the Amazon MP3 music player; video in the Amazon Video player; and docs, books, and magazines in the Kindle e-reader.

 When you first begin using Kindle Fire, before you've accessed any content, by default the Carousel contains the Amazon Kindle User Guide and the absolutely free New Oxford American Dictionary. It may also contain recently used content from your Amazon Cloud library.

Figure 2-10: Kindle Fire's Carousel makes recently used content available.

To remove an item from the Carousel, press and hold your finger on it; then tap Remove from Carousel from the menu that appears.

Organizing Favorites

When you're on a roll using Kindle Fire for accessing all kinds of content, the Carousel can get a bit crowded. You may have to swipe five or six times to find what you need. That's where Favorites comes in.

If, for example, you're reading a book you open often or you play a certain piece of music frequently, place

it in the Favorites area of the Kindle Fire Home screen
so you can find it more quickly.

By default, Favorites includes an Amazon Store app,
Pulse (a news aggregator app), the IMDb movie database app, and the Facebook app. To pin an item to
Favorites, press and hold it in the Carousel or a
library, and then select Add to Favorites from the
menu that appears (see Figure 2-11).

Figure 2-11: Pin items to Favorites by using this menu.

To remove content from Favorites, press and hold the
item, and then choose Remove from Favorites or
Delete from the menu that appears. Remove from
Favorites unpins the item from Favorites, although

it's still available to you on the Carousel and in the related library. Delete removes the item from the device (although it's still archived in Amazon's Cloud).

Getting clues from the Status bar

The Status bar runs across the top of every Kindle Fire screen, just like the Status bar on your mobile phone. This bar, shown in Figure 2-12, provides information about your battery charge and running apps, but it also provides access to the Kindle Fire settings.

Mary's 2nd kindle   11:24   ⚙ 📶 🔋

Figure 2-12: Tools and settings available on the Status bar.

Here's a rundown of what you'll find on the Status bar:

✔ **Device name:** First is the name of your Kindle Fire, such as Mary's Kindle or Mary's 2nd Kindle.

✔ **Notifications:** A number sometimes appears next to the name of your device to indicate that you have that many Notifications. Notifications can come from the Kindle Fire system announcing a completed download or the e-mail client announcing that a new e-mail has arrived, for example. To view all your notifications, tap the Notifications icon, and a list appears (see Figure 2-13).

✔ **Current time:** The next item on the Status bar is the current time, based on the time zone you specified when setting up the Kindle Fire.

✔ **Quick Settings:** Jumping to the right side of the Status bar, you first encounter a spoked-wheel-shaped icon that you tap to access Quick Settings. Quick Settings offers the most commonly used settings. Use these items to adjust volume, brightness, or your Wi-Fi connection, for example. To access the full Kindle Fire Settings menu, tap More (see Figure 2-14).

✔ **Wi-Fi Connection:** The item on the Status bar to the right of Quick Settings is an icon showing you the Wi-Fi connection status. If this is lit up, you're connected. The more bars in the symbol that are bright white, the stronger the connection.

✔ **Battery charge:** Finally, there's an icon that indicates the percentage of charge remaining on your battery.

Figure 2-13: The list of current notifications that you can display from any screen.

The Options bar

The Options bar runs along the bottom of your Kindle Fire screen. The items offered on the Options bar change, depending on what library or app you're using, but they always include a Home button. Also, there are often items such as Search to run a search in features such as a content library. In addition, you'll almost always see a Menu button when you tap the Options bar. This icon makes available commonly used actions, such as those for accessing settings for the currently displayed feature. Figure 2-15 shows you the options available on the Music library screen.

Figure 2-14: Use the Quick Settings menu or tap More to access the full complement of settings for Kindle Fire.

Use the Home button to jump back to the Kindle Fire from anywhere. On some screens where it would be annoying to be distracted by the Options bar, such as the e-reader, you may have to tap the bottom of the screen to make the Options bar appear.

Home button   Search

Menu button

Figure 2-15: The Options bar offers contextually relevant options, depending on which screen is displayed.

Using a Micro-B Cable to Transfer Data

It's easy to purchase or rent content from Amazon, which you can choose to download directly to your Kindle Fire or stream from Amazon Cloud. However, you may want to get content from other places, such as iTunes or your Pictures folder on your computer, and play or view it on your Kindle Fire.

To transfer content to Kindle Fire, you have to use a micro-B cable. This cable has a USB connector on one end that you can plug into your PC or Mac, and a micro-B connector on the other that fits into the slot on your Kindle Fire (which is located next to the Power button).

You can buy a micro-B cable from Amazon for about $10 or search for a cable from other sources, if you like (as long as there's a USB connector on one end and a micro-B connector on the other, it should work with your Kindle Fire).

When you get the cable, attach the micro-B end to your Kindle Fire and the USB end to your computer. Your Kindle Fire should then appear as a drive in Windows Explorer or the Mac Finder. You can now click and drag files from your hard drive to the Kindle Fire or use the copy and paste functions to accomplish the same thing.

Using this process, you can transfer apps, photos, docs, music, e-books, and videos from your computer to your Kindle Fire. Then, just tap the relevant library (such as Books for e-books and Music for songs) to read or play the content on your Kindle Fire.

 You can also upload content to your Amazon Cloud library on your computer, and that content will then be available on your Kindle Fire from the Cloud. See Chapter 6 for more about how this process works.

Chapter 3

Kindle Fire Settings

• •

In This Chapter

▶ Opening your Kindle Fire's settings

▶ Working with Quick Settings

▶ Delving into the Kindle Fire settings

• •

*W*hen you first take your Kindle Fire out of the box, Amazon has provided you with default settings that will work for most people most of the time. However, you can personalize the settings to make Kindle Fire work uniquely for you.

Some of these settings are discussed in the chapters that cover individual apps, such as the Amazon video player (Chapter 6). I cover the more general settings in this chapter.

Opening Quick Settings

In this fast-paced day and age, quick is the name of the game for most of us. So Amazon has provided you with Quick Settings to streamline your settings experience.

You access both a short list of commonly used settings and all the more detailed settings for Kindle Fire by tapping the Quick Settings button in the Status bar. (This button looks like the spokes of a wheel and is located toward the top-right corner of the screen.)

Here are the settings that you can control from the Quick Settings menu (see Figure 3-1):

- **Unlocked/Lock:** This is a toggle feature, meaning that you tap it to lock your device, which displays a black screen, and then you tap the setting again to unlock it, which displays the Home screen.

- **Volume:** Tap Volume to display a slider bar that you can use to increase or decrease the volume (see Figure 3-2).

- **Brightness:** You can tap and display Automatic Brightness On/Off buttons to turn on or off a feature that controls the brightness of the screen based on ambient light. You can also use the slider beneath this setting (see Figure 3-3) to adjust the brightness manually.

Figure 3-1: Quick Settings control the settings that you access most often.

Figure 3-2: Controls that appear when you tap Volume.

Figure 3-3: Adjust brightness manually by using this slider.

✔ **Wi-Fi:** Tap to display an On/Off button (see Figure 3-4) that you can use to turn Wi-Fi on or off. When you turn Wi-Fi on, a list of available networks appears. Tap an available network to join it. Note that you may be asked to enter a password to access some networks.

Figure 3-4: Choose from the list of available networks.

✔ **Sync:** Generally speaking, if you're within range of a Wi-Fi network, when you begin to download content, it downloads very quickly. However, if you've been out of range of a network, you might want to use this setting when you're back in range of a network to manually initiate the download of new content or continue downloads that may have been interrupted.

Finding Other Settings

Beyond what I discuss in the preceding section, there is one more item on the Quick Settings menu — More. Figure 3-5 shows you the many settings that appear when you tap the More button.

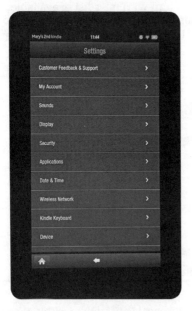

Figure 3-5: Plenty more settings are revealed when you tap More.

These settings include: Customer Feedback &
Support, My Account, Sounds, Display, Security,
Applications, Date & Time, Wireless Network, Kindle
Keyboard, Device, Legal Notices, and Terms of Use.

You won't need to change many of these settings very
often because the way Kindle Fire works out of the
box is usually very intuitive. But if you do find that
you want to make an adjustment to settings such as
the date and time, or security, it's useful to know
what's available.

The following sections give you the skinny on what
settings appear when you tap More in the Quick
Settings menu.

Help & Feedback

When you tap Customer Feedback & Support from
Settings, you see the Help & Feedback screen, which
offers a world of help and allows you to interact with
Amazon customer service (see Figure 3-6).

The Help & Feedback screen includes three somewhat self-explanatory tabs: FAQ & Troubleshooting,
Contact Customer Service, and Feedback. The last
two tabs display a form in which you can type a message to send on to Amazon. Here's how these three
options work:

✔ **FAQ & Troubleshooting:** Use this tab, shown in
Figure 3-7, to get help with the following topics:
Registration, Home Screen and Navigation,
Books, Video, Docs, Web, Newsstand, and Other
Apps. There is also a More Online Help link to
connect you with additional Amazon resources.

Figure 3-6: Help & Feedback settings for Kindle Fire.

✔ **Contact Customer Service:** The first question
you have to answer here is "What can we help
you with?" Use the Select an Issue drop-down
list to locate a related issue and tap the Back
button. You can also tap the Select Issue Details
drop-down list, choose a more specific topic,
and then tap the Back button. Choose from the
How Would You Like to Contact Us field by
selecting either e-mail (tap the Send Us an
E-mail button) or phone (tap the Call Us
button).

Figure 3-7: This Frequently Asked Questions tab leads you to help on a variety of topics.

✔ **Feedback:** Tap Select a Feature and choose from the list that appears (items such as Newsstand, Books, Docs, and so on). Then, tap Back to go back to Feedback. Enter your comment in the Tell Us What You Think about This Feature field. You can also tap one to five stars to rate the feature you're providing feedback on (see Figure 3-8). Tap the Send Feedback button to submit your thoughts to Amazon.

Figure 3-8: The Feedback tab of Help & Feedback gives you a forum for your opinions.

My Account

Kindle Fire does much of what it does by accessing your Amazon account. You need to have an Amazon account to shop, access the Amazon Cloud library online, and register your Kindle Fire, for example.

The My Account option in Settings provides information about the account to which the device is registered (see Figure 3-9). To remove this account from your Kindle Fire, you can tap the Deregister button. Because the obvious thing to do next is to register your Kindle Fire to another account (because so much depends on your having an associated account), you then are presented with a Register button. Tap Register and fill in your Amazon user-name and password to register the device.

Figure 3-9: Check which Amazon account your device is registered to.

Controlling sounds

With a tablet that's so media-centric, it's important that you know how to control the volume. If you tap Sounds in Kindle Settings, you see two items (see Figure 3-10): a volume slider that you can use to move the volume up or down, and Notification Sounds. Notifications may come from the arrival of a new e-mail, a completed download, or an app notification (such as an appointment reminder from a calendar app that you may have downloaded). To modify Notification Sounds, tap the arrow on the right of this item and, from the list that appears, choose the sound you want to use.

Figure 3-10: Sound settings are pretty darn simple to use.

Managing the display

From within Settings, you can manage your device's display, adjusting both the screen brightness and how long it takes for the screen to lock when the device isn't being used. Tap Display, and you can work with these settings (see Figure 3-11):

- ✔ **Brightness:** Tap and drag the circle on this slider to the right to make the screen brighter and to the left to dim it.

- ✔ **Screen Timeout:** After a certain period of inactivity, the Kindle Fire screen will lock and go black to save battery power. You can adjust the length of this interval by tapping the arrow in this field and choosing from a list that ranges from 30 seconds to one hour. You can also choose the option Never if you want your screen to be always on. However, remember that using the Never option or a very long interval will wear down your battery.

Figure 3-11: Manage display controls.

Making security settings

The first thing you can do to keep your Kindle Fire secure is to never let it out of your hands. But because we can't control everything and sometimes things get lost or stolen, it's a good idea to assign a password that's required to unlock your Kindle Fire screen. If a thief or other person gets his hands on your Kindle

Fire, there's no way he can get at stored data, such as your Amazon account information or contacts.

Tap the Security Settings option, and you'll see three simple choices (see Figure 3-12):

✔ **Lock Screen Password On/Off:** Simply tap On, and fields appear labeled Enter Password and Confirm Password. Tap in the Enter Password field and, using the onscreen keyboard that appears, type a password. Tap in the Confirm Password field and retype the password. Tap Finish to save your new password.

✔ **Credential Storage:** Credentials are typically used for Microsoft Exchange–based accounts, such as an account you use to access e-mail on your company's server. If you use Microsoft Exchange, it's a good idea to get your network administrator's help to make the following settings: Install Secure Credentials, Set Credential Storage Password, Use Secure Credentials, and Clear Credential Storage.

✔ **Device Administrators:** If your device is being administered through a company Exchange account, use this setting to establish the device administrator who can modify settings for the account.

Figure 3-12: The Security settings offer three ways to secure your Kindle Fire.

You have to get an app if you want to set up
Kindle Fire to work with Microsoft Exchange
accounts. Try Exchange by Touchdown, which
you can get from the Amazon Appstore by tapping Apps on your Home screen.

Working with applications

Apps can help you do everything from manage e-mail
to play games. Managing the way apps work on your
Kindle Fire is done through the Applications settings.

When you tap Applications in Settings, you see a list
of installed apps, including the app that controls
Settings (see Figure 3-13). Tap any of these apps, and
you encounter the following options:

- ✔ **Force Stop:** Force Stop allows Kindle Fire to
  stop an application from running if it encounters
  problems.

- ✔ **Uninstall:** Uninstall removes the app from your
  Kindle Fire. Keep in mind, though, that although
  the app is uninstalled, if you purchased it from
  Amazon, it's still archived in the Cloud.

- ✔ **Storage:** You can clear Kindle Fire's memory of
  data stored by the app by tapping the Clear
  Data button.

- ✔ **Cache:** Computing devices store data based on
  your usage to more quickly provide the data
  you need. This so-called cache of data fills up a
  bit of memory, so if you want to free up some
  memory, tap the Clear Cache button.

- ✔ **Launch by Default:** Tap this button to launch an
  app automatically when you turn on Kindle Fire.

- ✔ **Permissions:** A list of permissions to allow access
  to information that this app might have to use to
  perform its function, such as your location.

Figure 3-13: Each application on your Kindle Fire has associated settings.

Adjusting date and time

You chose a Time Zone setting when you first set up
your Kindle Fire (see Chapter 2). Your Kindle Fire
uses the date and time setting to display the time in
the Status bar and to work with other apps, such as a
third-party calendar, for example. If you tap Date and
Time in Settings, you see the four options shown in
Figure 3-14:

✔ **Automatic:** If you want Kindle Fire to control the date and time based on your location, tap to turn this feature On. If you'd rather set the time manually, tap to turn this Off.

✔ **Set Time:** To manually set the time, after you turn the Automatic option Off, tap the arrow on the right of this setting to display additional settings (see Figure 3-15). Tap the + (plus sign) and – (minus sign) buttons to change the time, and then tap Save.

✔ **Set Date:** Tap the arrow to the right of Set Date and then tap the + (plus sign) and – (minus sign) buttons to set the date you want, and then tap Save.

✔ **Select Time Zone:** Tap the arrow to the right of this setting to change your time zone.

The Set Time settings become available only if you first turn the Automatic option to Off.

Figure 3-14: Let Kindle Fire control your time and date with the Automatic setting.

Figure 3-15: Manually set the time and date on your Kindle Fire.

Setting up Wi-Fi

Wi-Fi is a pretty essential setting for using Kindle Fire. Without a Wi-Fi connection, you can't stream video or music, shop at the various Amazon stores, or send and receive e-mail.

Tap Wireless Network to view these settings (see Figure 3-16):

- **Wireless Network:** Turn Wi-Fi on or off. With Wi-Fi on, you can then click an item in the list of available networks, and Kindle connects to that network.

- **Add a Network:** Tap this setting to enter a new network's SSID (the public name of a Wi-Fi network) and security information to add it to the list of available networks.

- **Advanced Settings:** Tap this option to reveal settings that allow you to enable international channels (the options here are Europe or Japan) if you're travelling overseas and want to access foreign Wi-Fi networks; or modify static IP settings. Static IP settings are most relevant if you're trying to access a corporate network, in which case, your network administrator can probably give you the specific settings to use.

Figure 3-16: Turn on and choose your preferred Wi-Fi network.

Working with the keyboard

There's no physical keyboard with your Kindle Fire, so you depend on its onscreen keyboard to provide input to apps such as Quickoffice, or in fields used to search and enter text into forms, such as e-mail messages.

There are three simple things you can do with Kindle Keyboard settings; all three offer the basic On/Off choices (see Figure 3-17):

- ✓ **Sound on Keypress:** If you like that satisfying clicky sound when you tap a key on the onscreen keyboard, tap to turn this setting on.

- ✓ **Auto-Capitalization:** If you want Kindle Fire to automatically capitalize proper names or the first word in a sentence, tap to turn this setting on.

- ✓ **Quick Fixes:** Turning this setting on allows Kindle Fire to correct common typing errors, such as typing *teh* when you mean *the*.

Figure 3-17: Control your onscreen keyboard with these settings.

Looking at device settings

You can check your Kindle Fire device settings (see Figure 3-18) to find out facts such as the remaining storage space available or your device's serial number. This is also where you can reset your Kindle Fire to the state it was in when it left the factory, if you like a clean slate now and then.

Here are the device settings available to you:

- ✔ **Storage:** Tells you how much memory is still available on your device.

- ✔ **Battery:** Indicates the percentage of battery power remaining.

- ✔ **System Version:** Relates to the operating system version for your Kindle Fire. New versions are released periodically, so if your version isn't the most current, you might need to update it by tapping the Update Your Kindle button (see Figure 3-19).

Figure 3-18: Device settings provide a lot of information about the status of your device.

Figure 3-19: Amazon occasionally provides system updates; you can update manually.

> ✓ **Serial Number:** Here's where you can find the serial number you might need to reference to interact with Amazon technical or customer support.

- ✔ **Wi-Fi MAC Address:** Every device that can connect to a Wi-Fi network has a unique address. This is where you can find yours.

- ✔ **Allow Installation of Applications:** Kindle Fire is set up to get its content from Amazon because that provides some measure of confidence and security. For example, apps you side-load from your computer to Kindle Fire that are from third-party suppliers are more likely to introduce viruses to your computer. Still, you can buy apps elsewhere and port them over from your computer. If you want to allow this, choose On in this setting. If you don't want to let apps other than those verified by Amazon to be placed on your Kindle Fire, tap Off.

- ✔ **Reset to Factory Defaults:** This setting could come in handy in a couple of situations. If you sold your Kindle Fire to somebody (so you can buy a newer version, of course!), you wouldn't want that person to have your docs and contact information. Also, if you've loaded a lot of content on your Kindle Fire and then decide you want a clean beginning to clear up memory, you might choose to reset the device. Resetting wipes all content and any changes you've made to default settings. If you tap this setting, you see the confirming dialog box shown in Figure 3-20. Tap Erase Everything to continue with the reset procedure or Cancel to close the warning dialog box and halt the reset.

Although you get 8GB of storage with Kindle Fire, a chunk of that is taken up in pre-installed and system files. So the storage available may indicate that you have something like 6.5GB of total storage available on the device.

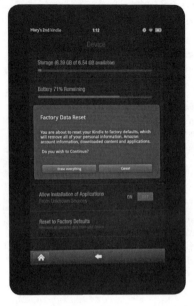

Figure 3-20: Be sure you want to reset before you accept this option.

Chapter 4

Going Shopping

• •

In This Chapter

▶ Using your Amazon account

▶ Shopping at the Amazon Appstore

▶ Buying apps, music, video, and print

▶ Buying other Amazon items through your Kindle Fire

• •

*A*mazon offers both a rich supply of books, maga-zines, music, and video, and an Amazon Appstore that you can use to get your hands on apps that add to the functionality of your Kindle Fire. These apps can range from simple utilities such as a calculator to fun and addictive games and even a word processor or spreadsheet.

In this chapter, you discover how to get apps, as well as books and other content for your Kindle Fire.

Managing Your Amazon Account

You buy things from Amazon by using the account and payment information you provide when you create an Amazon account. You probably have an account if you ever bought anything on Amazon (or opened an account when you bought your Kindle Fire). To buy things on Amazon with your Kindle Fire, you need to have associated your Amazon account with your Kindle Fire, which happens during the setup process covered in Chapter 2.

After you associate your device with an Amazon account, you manage account settings by going to the Amazon website by using the browser on either your Kindle Fire or computer and then tapping or clicking (depending on whether you're using a touchscreen device) Your Account in the top-right corner of the Amazon screen. You can then tap/click Manage Payment Options or Add a Credit or Debit Card from the Payment section of your account, and then change or enter a new method of payment and billing address.

Visiting the Amazon Appstore

After you create an Amazon account (which I discuss in the preceding section), you can shop for all kinds of content from your Kindle Fire. I'll start by introducing you to the world of apps.

Apps provide you with functionality of all kinds, from an app that turns your Kindle Fire into a star-gazing instrument to game apps. You can find calendar apps, drawing apps, and apps that provide maps so that you can find your way in the world.

Exploring the world of apps

You can buy apps for your Kindle Fire by using the Amazon Appstore. This store is full of apps written especially for devices that are based on the Android platform, including Kindle Fire.

 Android devices may have slightly different operating systems, and therefore not every app will work on every device. See Chapter 7 for some suggested apps that will work well with your Kindle Fire.

Follow these steps to explore the world of apps:

1. **Tap the Apps button at the top of the Home screen to enter your Apps library.**

2. **Tap the Store button.**

   The store shown in Figure 4-1 appears.

   At the top of the store is the offer *Get a Paid App for Free Every Day.*

3. **(Optional) Tap this option to download a free app to your device.**

Figure 4-1: The Amazon Appstore.

Below the free app offer are tabs. The tab labeled Top contains the most popular apps (this tab is active when you first open the store). Additional tabs include

- **New:** This tab displays the latest apps that have been added to the store.

- **Games:** Tap this tab to see featured game titles, as shown in Figure 4-2. Across the top of the Games section of the store are tabs such as Action, Adventure, Arcade, Board, Cards, Casino, Casual, Educational, Kids, Multiplayer, Music, Puzzles & Trivia, Racing, Role Playing, and Sports.

- **Entertainment:** Here, you'll find entertainment-related apps such as the IMDb movie database app or Old Time Radio Player. Three tabs — All, Top, and Recommended for You — help you browse for content.

- **Lifestyle:** This category includes apps for managing various areas of your life, such as home design and relationships. Across the top are tabs including Home & Garden, Self Improvement, Astrology, Relationships, Hair & Beauty, Celebrity, Quizzes & Games, Advice, and Parenting.

- **News & Weather:** Tap this tab to see apps that help you keep on top of the latest news and weather information. Across the top are tabs including World, U.S. Newspapers, Business, Politics, Entertainment, Sports, Science & Tech, Health, and Weather.

- **Utilities:** These apps help you maintain your Kindle Fire and organize your life. Across the top are tabs including Battery Savers, Alarms & Clocks, Calculators, Calendars, and Notes.

- **Social Networking:** Use this tab to find social networking apps for services such as Facebook and LinkedIn.

Figure 4-2: Games includes puzzles, cards, sports, and more.

 On the bar containing categories, you are able to view only the beginning of the News & Weather category. Press your finger on the farthest right of this category bar and swipe to the left to reveal the last few categories listed above.

 You can also tap the Top tab to see the best-selling apps in each category, tap the All Categories tab to view all apps, or tap the Recommended for You tab to see recommendations in that category based on your buying history.

Searching for apps

You can have fun browsing through categories of apps, but if you know which app you want to buy, using the search feature can take you right to it.

To search for an app, follow these steps:

1. **Tap in the Search field.**

   The keyboard shown in Figure 4-3 appears.

Figure 4-3: Use the search field and onscreen keyboard in the Appstore to find what you want.

2. **Using the onscreen keyboard, enter the name of an app, such as the game Angry Birds Rio.**

   Suggestions appear beneath the Search field.

3. **Tap a suggestion to display the list of suggestions with more detailed results.**

4. **Tap an app name to see more details about it.**

   The Product Info screen appears, as shown in Figure 4-4. Read the description or tap the Photos, Reviews, or Recommendations tabs across the top of the screen to find out more about the app.

Figure 4-4: Product details are shown in the Product Info screen.

The Save button adds the app to your Saved for
Later list. You access this list by tapping the
Menu button on the Options bar, tapping More,
and then tapping Saved for Later. You can go to
this list at any time to buy an item or delete it
from the list by pressing and holding your finger
on it and then tapping Remove in the menu that
appears.

Buying apps

You might find something you want to own by browsing or searching, but however you find it, when you're
ready to buy, you can follow these steps:

1. **From the product description, tap the Price
   button.**

   Note that if the app is free, this button reads
   Free, but if you have to pay for the app, the app
   price (such as $0.99) is displayed on the button.
   When you tap the button, its label changes to
   Buy App (for paid apps) or Get App (for free
   apps).

2. **Tap the button again to purchase paid apps and
   download paid or free apps to your Kindle Fire.**

   A Downloading button appears, showing the
   download progress. When the installation is
   complete, an Open button appears.

3. **If you want to use the app immediately, tap the
   Open button.**

To use the app at any time, locate it in the App library
or, if you've used it recently, on the Carousel; tap the
app to open it. Each app has its own controls and settings, so look for a settings menu like the one for the
Angry Birds Rio game, shown in Figure 4-5.

Settings

Figure 4-5: App settings for Angry Birds Rio.

 You can also buy apps from the Appstore on your PC or Mac. When placing the app in your shopping cart, be sure to select Kindle Fire for the device you want to download the app to in the drop-down list below the Add to Cart button. When you complete your purchase, the app is immediately downloaded to your Kindle Fire.

To delete an installed app from your App library, press and hold it until a menu appears. Tap Remove from Device. The app isn't gone. It's still stored in the Cloud, and you can download it again at any time by tapping it in the Cloud tab of the App library.

Buying Content

From Amazon, you can buy publications, books, music, and video (movies and TV shows) to download or stream to your Kindle Fire. The buying process is somewhat similar for the different types of content, but there are slight variations, which I explain in the following sections.

Buying publications

Kindle Fire's color display makes browsing through color magazines especially appealing. If you tap Newsstand on the Home page of Kindle Fire, and then tap the Store button, you see several categories of items (see Figure 4-6).

Free Trials are displayed across the top. You can swipe right to left to scroll horizontally.

Figure 4-6: The Newsstand Store.

Below Free Trials, you see categories such as Featured Magazines, Featured Newspapers, and Fashion & Entertainment (the categories may change on a regular basis). Tap the See All button above any category to see a more complete list of included items.

When you find the publication you want, follow these steps to buy or subscribe to it:

1. **Tap the item.**

   A screen appears showing pricing, a description of the publication, and Subscribe Now and Buy Current Issue buttons.

2. **Tap Subscribe Now or Buy Current Issue.**

   The button label changes to read Downloading. When the download is complete, the button label changes to Read Now.

3. **Tap the Read Now button to open the magazine.**

   Note that the magazine is stored in your Amazon Cloud library, where you can read or download it to your Kindle Fire at a later time.

Buying books

If you've joined the electronic book revolution (or even if you haven't), you'll find that reading books on Kindle Fire is convenient and economical (e-books are typically a few dollars less than the print version, and you can borrow e-books from your local library for free).

To browse through e-books from Amazon on your Kindle Fire, follow these steps:

1. **Tap the Books button on the Kindle Fire Home screen.**

2. **Tap the Store button.**

   The Amazon Bookstore sports a Recommended for You section at the top, recommending books based on your buying history.

3. **Swipe right to left to scroll horizontally through the recommendations at the top.**

   You also see categories such as Top 100 Paid, Top 100 Free, and New & Noteworthy.

As with the Newsstand, when you locate and tap an item in the bookstore, you see a screen with that item's pricing and description (see Figure 4-7). In the bookstore, the buttons you see at this point are labeled Try a Sample and Buy (or Buy for Free). Here's how these two buttons work:

- **Try A Sample:** Tap this button, and it changes to a Downloading button, and then to a Read Sample Now button. Tap the Read Sample Now button to open the sample of the book.

- **Buy or Buy for Free:** Tap this button, and it changes to a Downloading button. When the download is complete, the button label changes to Read Now. Tap the Read Now button to open the book. Remember that the book is now stored in your Books library, where you can tap it to open and read it at your leisure.

After you've read a bit of your new book, it will appear both in your Books library and on the Carousel on the Home screen.

 To remove a book from your device (remembering that it will still be stored in the Amazon Cloud), open your Book library, press and hold the book, and tap Remove from Device from the menu that appears.

Figure 4-7: Details about a book in the Amazon Bookstore.

Buying music

No matter what kind of music you prefer, from hip-hop to Broadway, you're likely to find a great many selections tucked away in Amazon's vaults.

Tap the Music button on the Kindle Fire Home screen and then tap the Store button. At the top of the Store screen, you see the following tabs: Featured, Bestsellers, New Releases, and Genres. Tap one of these tabs to get a list of items in that category (see Figure 4-8). You can also tap the Albums or Songs tabs to view music by these criteria.

Figure 4-8: The Amazon Music Store.

Below these tabs on the Music Store home page, you'll see thumbnails of music selections. Follow these steps to buy music:

1. **Tap an item.**

   A screen appears, displaying a list of the songs in the case of an album with Price buttons for both the entire album and each individual song.

2. **Tap the arrow button to the left of a song to play a preview of it.**

3. **Tap a Price button.**

   The button label changes from the price of the item to the word Buy.

4. **Tap the Buy button.**

   The song or album downloads to your Music library. A confirmation dialog box opens, displaying a Go to Your Library button and a Continue Shopping button (see Figure 4-9).

5. **Tap the Go to Your Library button to open the album and display the list of songs.**

   The album is now stored both in your Music library and the Cloud; if you tap on a song to play it, it'll also appear with recently accessed content in the Carousel.

Figure 4-9: This dialog box allows you to return to your library or keep shopping.

If you tap the Continue Shopping button, you can later find the album in your Music library.

See Chapter 6 for more about playing music.

Buying video

You should definitely check out the experience of consuming your video programs on a portable device such as Kindle Fire. From lying in bed or on the beach to watching your videos while waiting in line at the bank, portability can be a very convenient feature.

When you tap Video on the Kindle Fire Home screen, you're instantly taken to the Amazon Video Store shown in Figure 4-10.

Figure 4-10: Shop for video in the Amazon Video Store.

Across the top of the screen, you see thumbnails of items in the Prime Instant Videos category. Beneath these thumbnails is a horizontally scrolling list of thumbnails for movies from $2.99. Beneath this list are thumbnails of items in the category of TV Shows from $1.99.

Tap an item, and a descriptive screen appears. For TV shows, this screen includes episode prices and a set of Season tabs. For movies, this screen offers Watch Trailer, Purchase Options, and 48 Hour Rental buttons (see Figure 4-11).

Figure 4-11: The video screen offers several options.

Tap an episode Price button or a movie Purchase Options button, and the button becomes a Watch Now button. Tap the Watch Now button, and the TV show or movie starts to play.

Tap the 48 Hour Rental button for movies, and you see a Rent button. Tap this, and you're immediately charged for the rental. The 48-hour rental period begins when you start to watch the movie.

See Chapter 6 for more about playing videos.

Shopping for Anything Else

Amazon kindly pre-installed an Amazon Shopping app on your Kindle Fire so that you can quickly go to their online store and buy anything your heart desires.

The Amazon Shopping app is included in your Favorites right out of the box. Just tap it, and Amazon opens in your browser with a list of recommendations for you, based on previous purchases. You can tap the Shop All Departments tab to access a drop-down list of available departments.

Now, just proceed to shop as you usually do on Amazon, tapping any item of interest to add it to your cart and using your Amazon account information to pay and arrange for shipping.

Chapter 5

Getting Online

· ·

In This Chapter

▶ Using Wi-Fi on your Kindle Fire

▶ Browsing the web with Silk

▶ Personalizing Silk's settings

▶ Setting up e-mail

· ·

Kindle Fire can become your new go-to device for keeping informed and in touch by using Amazon's Silk browser and the pre-installed e-mail client.

In this chapter, you discover the ins and outs of browsing with Silk and the simple tools you can use to send and receive e-mail on Kindle Fire.

Getting Online by Using Wi-Fi

Kindle Fire is a Wi-Fi device, meaning that you have to have access to a nearby Wi-Fi network to go online. You might access a Wi-Fi connection through your home network, at work, or via a public hotspot, such as an Internet café or airport.

When you first set up your Kindle Fire (as described in Chapter 2), you can choose a Wi-Fi network to use for going online. If you want to log on to a different network, follow these steps:

1. **Tap Quick Settings to open a menu of common settings, such as Volume, Wi-Fi, and Brightness.**

2. **Tap Wi-Fi.**

    Wi-Fi settings appear (see Figure 5-1).

3. **Tap a network in the list of available wireless networks to sign in.**

    You have to enter a password to sign in to some networks.

 To set a password to block access to a Wi-Fi connection, tap Quick Settings from the Home screen, tap Wi-Fi, tap the Wi-Fi connection you want, and enter a password in the Password box. Tap Save to apply the password setting.

Browsing with Silk

Silk is a brand new browser from Amazon and takes advantage of Amazon's ability to use its own servers to make your browsing experience fast.

For example, if you visit a popular news website and choose to tap the headline story to get more details, the odds are many thousands of people have done the same thing. The Silk browser recognizes this pattern and holds that next page in its cache (a dedicated block of memory) to deliver it quickly to you if you also make this selection. This ability makes your browsing experience fast and smooth as, well, silk.

Figure 5-1: Use Wi-Fi settings to select a network to join.

In the following sections, I introduce you to Silk's browser environment. Many tools and features will be familiar to you from other browsers, but a few are unique to Silk.

Using navigation tools

Tap on the Web button at the far right of the library tools displayed across the top of the Kindle Fire Home screen to see Silk, as shown in Figure 5-2.

Address/Search field

Bookmarks button

Menu button

Forward button

Back button

Figure 5-2: Silk offers a familiar browser interface.

You can use the Back and Forward buttons to move among pages you've previously viewed. To go directly to a page, tap in the Address field (note that this field will act as a Search field if you enter a word or phrase or as an Address field if you enter a website's address, or URL). Enter a site address and tap Go. The website is displayed.

Silk uses tabs that allow you to display more than one web page at a time and move among those pages. Tap the Add Tab button — which features a plus sign (+) — to add a tab in the browser. When you do, thumbnails of recently visited sites appear. You can tap on a thumbnail to go to that site, or you can tap in the Address bar and enter a URL by using the onscreen keyboard that appears.

Bookmarking sites

You can bookmark sites in Silk so that you can easily jump back to those sites again. With a site displayed on screen, tap the Menu icon in the Options bar and tap Add Bookmark. In the Add Bookmark dialog box that appears (see Figure 5-3), tap OK to bookmark the currently displayed page. You can then tap the Bookmarks button shown in Figure 5-2 to display thumbnails of all bookmarked pages. Tap on one to go there.

Figure 5-3: Bookmarks help you return to a favorite page.

To delete a bookmark, after tapping the Bookmarks button to display thumbnails of bookmarked pages, press and hold a page. In the menu that appears, tap Delete. In the confirming dialog box that appears, tap OK and the bookmark is removed.

 When a website is open in Silk, the Menu button on the Options bar also provides a Share Page feature. When you tap this option, you can select to share the current page via Facebook or send a link to a page by using Amazon Email.

Searching for content on a page

Web pages can contain a lot of content, so it's not always easy to find the article or discussion you want to view on a particular topic. Most browsers provide a feature to search for content on a web page, and Silk is no exception.

To search the currently displayed page by using Silk, follow these steps:

1. **Tap Menu on the Options bar.**

2. **On the screen that appears (see Figure 5-4), tap Find in Page.**

   The onscreen keyboard appears with the Search field active.

3. **Type a search term.**

   It appears in an orange box hovering above the first instance of the word on the page. Other instances of the word on that page are highlighted by a white bubble outlined in orange, as shown in Figure 5-5.

Figure 5-4: Search the currently displayed page.

4. **Tap any of these bubbles to view the related content.**

5. **Tap Done to end the search.**

Searching the web

Search engines make our lives easier because they help us narrow down what we're looking for by using specific search terms; they then troll the web to find matches for those terms from a variety of sources.

First instance of word.

Figure 5-5: The first instance of a word on a page is indicated by an orange box.

To search the entire web, follow these steps:

1. **Tap the plus sign (+) to add a tab in the browser if you want search results to appear on a new tab.**

   Thumbnails of recently visited sites appear.

2. **Tap in the Search field.**

   The thumbnails change to a list of bookmarked sites, and the onscreen keyboard appears.

3. **Enter a Search term and tap Go.**

   Search results appear in Google.

4. **Tap a result to go to that page.**

 To specify a search engine to use other than the default, Google, tap the Menu button in the Options bar, and then tap Settings. Use the Set Search Engine option to choose Google, Bing, or Yahoo! as the default search engine.

Reviewing browsing history

We've all experienced this: You know you visited a site in the last day or so that had a great deal, product, news story, or whatever — but you just can't remember the URL of the site. That's where the ability to review your browsing history comes in handy. Using this feature, you can scan the sites you visited recently organized by day and, more often than not, spot the place you want to revisit.

With Silk open, tap the Menu button on the Options bar. Tap History, and sites you've visited on the Kindle Fire appear in a list divided into categories such as Today and Last 7 Days. Look over these sites and, when you find the one you want, tap it to go there.

Working with web page content

There are a few things you can do to work with contents of websites using Kindle Fire. For example, you may find online content that you want to download, such as a PDF file that you download to your Docs library or an image you download to the photo Gallery. You can also open or share content you find online.

Here's how these work:

- **View downloads.** Tap Menu on the Options bar, and then tap the Downloads button to view completed downloads.

- **Save or view images.** Press and hold an image, and a menu appears offering the option to Save Image or View Image (see Figure 5-6).

- **Open, save, or share links.** Press and hold your finger on any linked text until a menu appears offering these options: Open, Open in New Tab, Bookmark Link, Save Link, Copy Link URL, and Share Link.

Figure 5-6: You can work with links and images on your Kindle Fire by using this menu.

Personalizing Silk

Silk sports a nice, clean interface. Still, there are a few things you can do to personalize the way Silk looks and acts that might work better for you.

With Silk open, tap the Menu button on the Options bar, and then tap Settings. The screen that appears lists some of the things you can control about the Silk interface:

- ✔ **Text Size:** To make text on the page more readable, you might want to change the default size of text. Tap Text Size, and then choose Tiny, Small, Normal, Large, or Huge from the menu that appears

- ✔ **Default Zoom:** Specify Silk's default size of the view as Far, Medium, or Close.

 You can also double-tap a page to enlarge the view and double-tap again to reduce the view. Or with your fingers pinched together on the screen, spread them out to enlarge the view. Start with your fingers spread apart and then pinch them together to reduce the view size.

- ✔ **Auto-Fit Pages:** Formats web pages to automatically fit the screen.

- ✔ **Load Images:** Allows images on web pages to be displayed in the browser.

- ✔ **Open in Background:** Select this checkbox to open new tabs behind the current tab, rather than in front of it.

 You can get rid of all the personalized settings you've made to Silk. With Silk open, on the Options bar, tap the Menu button and then Settings. Scroll down to Advanced Settings, and then tap Reset to Default.

Making Privacy Settings

The Privacy settings for Silk help you to stay safe when you're browsing online. Tap the More button on the Options bar, and then tap Settings to view and modify the following privacy settings (see Figure 5-7):

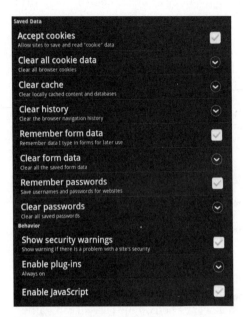

Figure 5-7: Privacy settings can protect your personal information as you browse.

- ✔ **Accept Cookies.** Tap this checkbox to stop sites from downloading cookies to your Kindle Fire.
- ✔ **Clear All Cookie Data.** You can tap this setting, and then in the Clear dialog box that appears, tap OK to clear all cookies from your device.
- ✔ **Clear Cache.** Any computing device holds information in its cache to help it redisplay a page you've visited recently, for example. To clear out that cache, which can also free up some memory on your Kindle Fire, tap OK.

✔ **Clear History.** Your Silk browser retains a history of your browsing activity to make it easy for you to revisit a site. However, it's possible for others who view your browsing history to draw conclusions about your online habits. To clear your history, tap OK in this setting.

✔ **Remember Form Data.** If you want Silk to remember data you've entered into forms before — such as your name, mailing address, or e-mail address — to help you complete online fields more quickly, tap this checkbox. The danger here, and the reason you might choose to deselect this checkbox, is that if somebody gets a hold of your Kindle Fire, they could use this feature to gain access to some of your personal information or use your online accounts.

✔ **Clear Form Data.** Clears out any form data you've already saved.

✔ **Remember Passwords.** If you want Silk to remember passwords that you enter for various accounts, tap this checkbox. Just be aware that this setting puts your accounts at risk should you ever misplace your Kindle Fire. One option, if you use this setting, is to require a password to unlock your Kindle Fire Home screen. This setting, which can help protect all content stored on the device, is discussed in Chapter 3.

✔ **Clear Passwords.** If you previously allowed Silk to remember passwords but have a change of heart, you can tap OK in this setting to remove saved passwords.

✔ **Show Security Warnings.** This is a handy feature that requires Silk to check for problems with a website you're trying to visit and warn you of any problems with the site. Tap the checkbox to activate the warnings.

- ✔ **Enable Plug-ins.** Tap this checkbox to allow plug-ins to run. *Plug-ins* are small programs that enable functionality in a web browser, such as displaying certain types of content.

- ✔ **Enable JavaScript.** JavaScript is used to run some scripts on web pages, but it has some rather legendary security gaps. Some people prefer not to enable JavaScript when they browse for this reason.

- ✔ **Block Pop-up Windows.** Tapping this setting opens a dialog box that offers the settings Ask, Never, and Always. You can choose to have Silk ask you whether it should open pop-up windows, never allow pop-ups at all, or always allow pop-ups by tapping the relevant setting.

Working with E-Mail

Kindle Fire has a built-in e-mail client that allows you to access e-mail accounts you've set up through various providers, such as Gmail and Windows Live Hotmail. You can then open the inboxes of these accounts and read, reply to, and forward messages by using your Kindle Fire. You can also create and send new messages, and even include attachments.

In the following sections, I provide information about setting up and using your e-mail accounts on Kindle Fire.

Setting up an e-mail account

Setting up your e-mail on Kindle Fire involves providing information about one or more e-mail accounts that you've already established with a provider such as Gmail.

Follow these steps to set up an e-mail account the first time you use the app:

1. **Tap Apps.**

   The Apps library appears.

2. **Tap Email.**

   The Email app opens and displays a Start button the first time you open the app.

3. **Tap the Start button.**

   A list of account types appears.

4. **Tap Gmail, Yahoo, Hotmail, AOL, or Other.**

   The dialog box shown in Figure 5-8 appears.

5. **Enter your username and password in the appropriate fields, and then tap Next.**

   A new screen appears, displaying two fields.

6. **Enter the name that will appear on outgoing messages in the Display Name field and a name in the Account Name field to identify the account for yourself.**

   The Account Name is optional.

7. **Tap the Send Mail from This Account by Default check box if you want to set this up as your default e-mail account.**

8. **Tap the View your Inbox button to go to the inbox for the account you just set up.**

You can set up as many e-mail accounts as you like. When you open the Kindle Fire Email app, you see a Unified Inbox that combines messages from all accounts you set up, as well as individual inboxes for each account (see Figure 5-9).

Figure 5-8: The screen for setting up your e-mail account.

 To delete an account in the Email app, tap the Menu button in the Options bar and then tap Accounts. Press and hold your finger on an account; from the menu that appears, tap Remove Account.

Sending e-mail

After you set up your e-mail account(s), as described in the preceding section, you're able to send e-mails from your Kindle Fire. To create and send an e-mail, with the Email app open, follow these steps:

Figure 5-9: Your Kindle Fire e-mail client inboxes.

1. **Tap the Compose icon.**

   This icon is the symbol of a small box and pencil at the bottom of the screen, to the left of the Search button.

   A blank e-mail form appears.

2. **In the To: field, enter a name.**

   Alternatively, tap the Add Contacts button, which features a plus sign (+), to open the Contacts app and tap on a name there to add that person as an addressee.

3. **If you want to send a copy of the e-mail to somebody, tap the Cc/Bcc button to make those fields appear; then enter addresses or choose them from the Contacts app by tapping the Add Contacts button.**

4. **Tap in the Subject field and enter a subject by using the onscreen keyboard.**

5. **Tap in the Message text field and enter a message.**

6. **(Optional) If you want to add an attachment to an e-mail, tap the Attach button shown at the bottom of the screen and, in the menu that appears, choose to attach an item from the photo Gallery or the Doc library.**

7. **To send your message, tap the Send button at the bottom of the screen.**

   If you decide you're not ready to send the message quite yet, you also have the option of tapping the Save Draft button and sending it later by tapping the Menu button on the Option bar from your Inbox, tapping Folders, and then opening the Drafts folder.

Here are a couple of handy shortcuts for entering text in your e-mail: The Auto Complete feature lists possible word matches as you type; tap one to complete a word. In addition, you can double-tap to place a period and space at the end of a sentence.

Receiving e-mail

Kindle Fire can receive your e-mail messages whenever you're connected to a Wi-Fi network.

When an e-mail is delivered to your inbox (see Figure 5-10), simply tap to open it. Read it and contemplate whether you want to save it or delete it (or forward or reply to it, as covered in the following section). If you don't need to keep the message, you can delete it by tapping the Trash button in the Options bar.

Forwarding and replying to e-mail

When you receive an e-mail, you can choose to reply to the sender, reply to the sender and anybody else who was included as an addressee on the original message, or forward the e-mail to another person.

Figure 5-10: Your inbox.

If you reply to all recipients, you send an answer
to the sender, anybody else in the To: field of
the original message, and anybody in the Cc:
and Bcc: fields. Because Bcc: fields aren't visible
to you as a recipient, you may be sending your
reply to people you're not aware of.

To forward or reply to an e-mail, with the Email app
inbox displayed, follow these steps:

1. **Tap an e-mail to open it.**

2. **Tap the Reply button.**

   A menu of options appears.

3. **Tap Reply, Reply All, or Forward.**

4. **If you're forwarding the message, enter a new recipient.**

   If you're replying, the message is already addressed, but you can enter additional recipients if you want to.

5. **Tap in the message area and enter your message.**

6. **Tap the Send button to send your message on its way.**

Sending E-Mail to Your Kindle Account

When you register your Kindle Fire, you get an associated e-mail account, which essentially allows you or others to e-mail documents in Word, PDF, RTF, or HTML format to your Kindle Fire.

The address of the account is displayed in the Docs library. Tap the Docs Library button on the Home screen, and you see a line that reads Send Documents to `YourE-MailAccount@kindle.com` where *Your E-Mail Account* is the name of your Kindle e-mail account.

You or others can e-mail documents to this address, and those documents automatically appear in your Docs library. Note that you might need to go to Amazon by using a browser and change the approved e-mail accounts. Click on Your Account and then on Manage Your Kindle. Click the Personal Document Settings and make sure the account is listed under Send to Kindle Email Settings as approved.

Chapter 6

Books, Videos, and Music

*T*his chapter is all about consuming content. Here, you discover what's available to read, how to open publications, and how to read and then delete them from Kindle Fire when you're finished. After talking about the Kindle e-reader, I explain how Amazon streams video content from the Cloud to your device. Then, I give you a look at the Kindle Fire Video library and cover the steps involved in playing a video. Finally, I show you how to get music onto your Kindle Fire (see Chapter 4 for more about shopping for music) and how to use the simple tools in the library to play your music.

E-Reader Extraordinaire

Kindle Fire comes from a family of e-readers, so it's only natural that the e-reader you use to read books and magazines on the device is a very robust feature. With its bright, colorful screen, Kindle Fire broadens your reading experience beyond black and white books to color publications such as magazines or graphic novels. The Kindle Fire's easy-to-use controls help you navigate publications, bookmark and high-light text, and search your libraries of print content.

So Many Things to Read!

Amazon started as an online book retailer, although through the years, it has branched out to become the largest retailer of just about everything on the planet. Kindle Fire makes it easy for you to buy your content from Amazon. Although you can buy and sideload content from other sources to Kindle Fire, buying from Amazon ensures that you're dealing with a repu-table company and receiving safe content (uncontam-inated by malware).

The content you buy from Amazon is automatically downloaded to your Kindle device, which means that not only is buying from Amazon's bookstore easy, but you can take advantage of its vast selection of books. In addition, you can borrow Kindle versions of books from many public libraries.

Amazon has also made deals to make many of your favorite magazines and newspapers available. With magazines and newspapers, you can buy the current issue or subscribe to get multiple issues sent to your Kindle Fire as they become available.

To buy books or magazines for your Kindle Fire, on the Home screen, tap either the Books or Newsstand button, which takes you to your Books or Magazine library.

Tap the Store button; this takes you to the Amazon Kindle bookstore, shown in Figure 6-1. (See Chapter 4 for more about how to search for and buy content.)

You can also buy content at the Amazon website from your computer and have it download to your Kindle Fire. Just select what device you want it delivered to from the drop-down list below the Add to Cart button before you buy Kindle content.

Figure 6-1: Buy magazines by the issue or subscribe by using Newsstand.

Reading Books

After you own some Kindle books, you can begin to read by using the simple e-reader tools in the Kindle e-reader app. You may have used this app on another device, such as your computer, smartphone, or tablet, although each version of this app has slightly different features. In the following sections, I go over the basics of how the Kindle e-reader app works on Kindle Fire.

 You can get to the Home screen from anywhere in the e-reader app. If a Home button isn't visible, just tap the bottom of the page to display the Options bar which includes a Home button and a set of tools for navigating a book.

Going to the (Books) library

When you tap Books on your Kindle Fire screen, you open the Books library, containing downloaded content on the Device tab and content in the Cloud on the Cloud tab (see Figure 6-2). The active tab is the one displaying orange text. There's also a Store button you use to go to Amazon's website and shop for books.

There are several features in your Books library that you can use to get different perspectives on its contents:

✔ **Grid and List views.** Tap Menu on the Options bar to display the Grid View and List View options. These provide views of your books by using large thumbnails on a bookshelf or in a text list including title and author, along with an accompanying small thumbnail.

- ✔ **Sort titles.** Use the By Author, By Recent, and By Title buttons to view books by any of these three criteria.

- ✔ **Identify new titles.** If you've just downloaded but haven't started reading a book, there will be a bright yellow banner in the corner of the thumbnail with the word New in it (see Figure 6-3).

Figure 6-2: The Books library displays all your book purchases on two tabs.

Tap the Search button on the Options bar to search your Books library contents by title or author.

Opening a book

To open a book from the Home screen, tap Books to open the Books library. Locate the book you want to read (swipe upward if you need to reveal more books in the list) and simply tap it. If the book has not been downloaded to your Kindle Fire, it begins to download and takes only seconds to complete.

New titles

Figure 6-3: New titles are easily identifiable.

If you've never begun to read the book, it opens on its title page. If you've read part of the book, it opens automatically to the last page you read. This last read page is bookmarked in the Cloud by Amazon when you stop reading, so no matter what device you use to read it — your Kindle Fire, computer, or smartphone, for example — you go to the last read page immediately.

 You can also open a publication from Favorites or the Carousel. Read more about these features in Chapter 2.

Navigating a book

The simplest way to move one page forward or one page back is to tap your finger anywhere on the right or left side of the page, respectively. Try this to move from the title page to a page of text within the book. With a book page displayed, tap it to see the tools shown in Figure 6-4, including a button to take you to the Kindle Fire Home screen, a Back button to go back one screen, a Font menu to make adjustments to the appearance of fonts and the page, a Menu button to access additional settings, and a Search button to initiate a search for text in the book.

Figure 6-4: Navigation tools in Kindle e-reader.

You can also tap the Menu icon in the Options bar and choose from these options to move around your book:

- ✔ **Cover:** Display the book cover.

- ✔ **Table of Contents:** Go to the table of contents if one is available for the current title; some children's books and novels, for example, have no table of contents.

- ✔ **Beginning:** Return to the beginning of the book.

- ✔ **Location:** Display the dialog box shown in Figure 6-5. Location is calculated by the number of bits of information in the book up to the current location. You can note the location of a particular page by checking this information above the progress bar at the bottom of any page. Tap in the location field and use the onscreen keyboard to enter that location, and then tap OK.

- ✔ **Sync to Furthest Page:** This option moves you to the last page you read in the book by using any Kindle reader apps or devices.

- ✔ **My Notes & Marks:** Opens a list showing the location of bookmarks, highlights, and notes that you've inserted into the book (see more about how to do this in the section "Bookmarking and highlighting," later in this chapter), as shown in Figure 6-6. Tap a selection to go that page.

The progress bar along the bottom of the screen indicates how far along in the publication you are at the moment. To move around the publication, you can press the circle on this bar and drag it in either direction.

Figure 6-5: Enter a location in the book to jump there instantly.

Searching in a book

Want to find that earlier reference to a character so that you can keep up with a plot? Or do you want to find any mention of Einstein in an e-encyclopedia? To find words or phrases in a book, use the Search feature.

Figure 6-6: A list of your bookmarks, highlights, and notes.

Follow these steps to search a book:

1. **With a book open, tap the page to display the Option bar, if necessary.**

2. **Tap the Search button in the Option bar.**

   The Search dialog box and onscreen keyboard are displayed.

3. **Enter a search term or phrase, and then tap the Search key on the keyboard.**

   Search results are displayed.

If you'd rather search the web, press a word or phrase to highlight it, and then in the resulting dialog box, tap the More button. At this point, you can tap either Search in Book, Search Wikipedia, or Search Google. The Google option takes you to search results for the term in the Google search engine, and the Wikipedia option takes you to the entry in the popular online encyclopedia that matches your search term. Tap the Back button when you want to return to the e-reader app.

Bookmarking and highlighting

If you find that perfect quote or a word you just have to read again at a later time, you can use the Highlight or Bookmark feature in Kindle e-reader.

To place a bookmark on a page, display the page and tap it to reveal the Bookmark button (a plus sign in the top-right corner of the page), and then tap the button. A small bookmark ribbon appears on the page (see Figure 6-7).

To highlight text, press and hold your finger on the text. Small handles appear on either side, as shown in Figure 6-8. If you want to select additional adjacent text to be highlighted, press your finger on one of these triangular handles and drag to the left or right. When the entire phrase or paragraph you want to highlight is selected, press the selected text to display a menu, and then tap Highlight.

Bookmark

Figure 6-7: A bookmarked page.

When you place a bookmark on a page or highlight text within a book, you can then display a list of book-marks and highlights by tapping the Menu button in the Option bar and choosing My Notes & Marks. You can jump to the page indicated by a bookmark or to highlighted text by tapping an item in this list.

When you press text and see the menu shown in Figure 6-8, a brief definition appears from the pre-installed New American Oxford Dictionary. In the definition window, tap Full Definition to go to the full Oxford dictionary definition. Tap the Back button to return to the book.

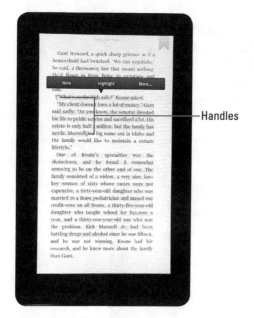

Handles

Figure 6-8: Click either handle to enlarge the area of selected text.

Modifying how a page looks

There are several things you can do to control how things appear on a page in Kindle e-reader. First, you can make text larger or smaller. Second, you can adjust the width of margins. You can also modify spacing between lines. Finally, you can choose a white, black, or sepia-toned background for a page.

To control all these settings, tap the page to display the Options bar, and then tap the Font button (the one with a capital and lowercase A). The options shown in Figure 6-9 appear:

- ✔ **Font Size:** Tap a particular font sample to change the size.

- ✔ **Line Spacing:** Choose how much space to put between lines.

- ✔ **Margins:** Choose the margin setting you prefer.

- ✔ **Color Mode (black on white, white on black, black on sepia):** Tap a setting to display a different color page background. A sepia background may make reading easier on your eyes, for example.

Figure 6-9: Font options offer you some control over the appearance of your pages.

You can adjust brightness manually or have Kindle Fire do it automatically. Tap the Quick Settings button at the top-right corner of the screen, and then tap the Brightness button. If you turn Automatic Brightness on, the Kindle Fire will adjust brightness of the screen to compensate for ambient light conditions. If you turn Automatic Brightness off, you can use the slider to adjust brightness. Press the circle on the slider and move it to the left or right to adjust brightness.

Managing publications

After you purchase content on Amazon, from apps to music and books, it's archived in your Amazon Cloud library. If you finish reading a book on Kindle Fire, you can remove it from your device. The book is still in the Amazon Cloud, and you can re-download it to your Kindle Fire at any time.

To remove a book or magazine from your Book library, follow these steps:

1. **Tap Books or Newsstand to display your library.**
2. **Locate and press your finger on the item.**

   A menu appears (see Figure 6-10).
3. **Tap Remove from Device.**

The thumbnail of the item remains in your Books library on the Cloud tab and on the Carousel or Favorites if you've placed it there. To download and read the book again, just double-tap it in any of these locations, and the download begins.

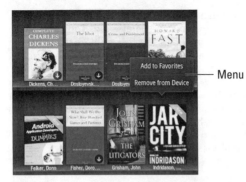

— Menu

Figure 6-10: Use this menu to remove a publication from Kindle Fire.

Unlike video and music, which you can stream from the Cloud without ever downloading them, books, magazines, and newspapers can't be read from the Cloud, they must be downloaded to a Kindle device before you can read them.

Reading Periodicals

Reading magazines and newspapers on your Kindle Fire is similar to reading books, with a few important differences. You navigate magazines a bit differently and can display them in two different views.

Follow these steps to read a magazine or newspaper:

1. **From the Home screen, tap Newsstand.**

2. **Tap a magazine or newspaper in the Newsstand to read it.**

   Alternatively, you can tap an item on the Carousel from the Home screen.

If the publication hasn't been downloaded to the device, it begins to download now.

With the Options bar visible, thumbnails of all pages in the publication are displayed along the bottom of the screen (see Figure 6-11).

3. **Swipe right or left to scroll through these pages, or drag the scroll bar indicator left or right.**

4. **When you find the page you want, tap that page to display it full screen.**

The Menu button on the Options bar displays contents of the current issue.

Figure 6-11: Scroll through thumbnails of pages to find the one you want.

5. **Tap an item in the table of contents to go to that item.**

 As with books, you can double-tap to enlarge text on the page; double-tap again to reduce the size of the text. You can also pinch and unpinch the touchscreen to move between larger and smaller views of a page's contents.

Some periodicals can appear in two views:

- ✔ **Text view:** In Text view, you see articles in more of an e-reader format (meaning that you get larger text with no columns and no images). In Text view, there's a Font button on the Options bar offering Font Style and Typeface tabs to adjust the size and font used for text. There's also a Style choice for changing Size, Spacing, Margins, and Color Mode (page background).

- ✔ **Page view:** Page view shows an exact image of the publication's pages, with all columns and photos intact. You can scroll through the magazine, view it in landscape or portrait orientation, and pinch and unpinch to zoom in and out of the pages.

Tap the Page View or Text View button in the top-right corner of a displayed periodical to switch between these views (if the periodical offers this feature).

Playing Videos

Playing video, both movies and TV shows, is a great use of Kindle Fire. The device has a bright, crisp screen, can easily be held in one hand, and is capable of streaming video from the Cloud, making a typically seamless viewing experience without hogging memory on the tablet itself.

In addition, Amazon offers an amazing selection of video content, including absolutely free Prime Instant Videos (as long as you maintain a Prime account with Amazon).

Streaming versus downloading

When you tap the Video button on the Kindle Fire Home screen, you're immediately taken to the Amazon Video Store (see Figure 6-12), rather than to a library of video titles. That makes sense because, by design, Kindle Fire is best used to stream videos from the Cloud. The device's relatively small memory (8GB) can't accommodate a large number of video files; instead, Amazon makes it easy for you to stream video to the device without ever downloading it. To go to your Video library, tap the Library button in the top-right corner.

Video content might include Prime Instant Videos, a feature which offers thousands of titles for free with an Amazon Prime account. (You get one free month of Amazon Prime with your Kindle Fire, after which you can purchase a membership for $79 a year.) You can also purchase or rent other video programs and stream them from the Cloud.

Amazon's Whispersync technology keeps track of the spot in a video where you stopped watching. You can later resume watching that video at that exact location on Kindle Fire, a PC or Mac, or one of over 300 compatible TVs, Blu-ray Disc players, or other devices.

You *can* download videos you purchase (you can't download Prime Instant Videos, however), which is useful if you want to watch them away from a Wi-Fi connection. It's a good idea to remove them from the device when you're done to save space. To delete a video from your device, open the Video library and tap the Device tab. Press and hold your finger on the video, and then tap Remove from Device in the menu that appears.

Looking at your video library

The Kindle Fire Video library may become your favorite destination for buying, viewing, and organizing your video content.

Figure 6-12: The Amazon Video Store offers thousands of titles.

When you tap Video on your Kindle Fire Home screen, the Amazon Video Store opens (refer to Figure 6-12).

The Store shows three video categories: Prime Instant Videos, Movies, and TV Shows. Tap any category name to see items in that category. When you display a category, on the screen that appears, there are Movies, Prime, All, and TV tabs that you can use to go to other categories.

 Tap the View All button in the Store to show all items organized by popularity.

Tap the Library button to go to your Video library (see Figure 6-13). The library sports two tabs — one lists all your videos stored in the Cloud, and one includes videos you've purchased that have been downloaded to the device. The tab that has orange lettering is the active tab.

In addition to the Cloud and Device tabs, there are tabs for filtering content by Movies or TV programs. Note that there's no search function you can use to find the content you're looking for.

Figure 6-13: The Kindle Fire Video library.

Downloaded video content is listed chronologically by the date you downloaded it.

Tap the Menu button on the Options bar to display two items — Settings and Help. In Settings (see Figure 6-14), you can view the Device ID and access the Disable HD Purchase Warning setting. If you disable this feature, it turns off a warning that tells you that, although you can play high-definition videos on Kindle Fire, they won't play in high definition because it's not a high-definition device.

Figure 6-14: You may want to disable this warning after seeing it once or twice.

 You can also use the By Recent and By Name buttons to view your video content by one of these sort criteria.

Opening and playing a video

Playing a video is a simple process. If the video has been downloaded to your device, open the library (tap Video, and then tap the Library button), locate the video (using methods described in the preceding section), and then tap the video to play it.

If you're streaming a video you've purchased from the Cloud, follow these steps:

1. **Tap the Cloud tab.**

   Videos you've rented (whose rental period hasn't expired) or purchased are displayed.

2. **Double-tap an item to open it.**

   If it's a TV show, you see episodes listed (see Figure 6-15); tap one to open it. If it's a movie, at this point, you see a description of the movie.

3. **Tap the Watch Now button.**

   The playback controls appear.

4. **If you've already watched part of the video, tap the Resume button.**

    If you'd rather see the video from its start, tap the Play from Beginning button.

   The movie appears full screen (see Figure 6-16). The title of the Movie appears at the top of the screen.

Figure 6-15: The episode list for a TV show.

Note that the Kindle Fire screen provides an extra-wide viewing angle. This means that you and those watching with you can see the content from the side as well as from straight on.

The familiar playback tools available here include

- ✔ Play
- ✔ Pause
- ✔ A progress bar
- ✔ A volume slider
- ✔ A button that moves you ten seconds back in the video

There's also a Back button in the Options bar that you can tap to stop playback and return to the Kindle Fire Video library. The More Episodes button goes back to all episodes of a TV show.

10 seconds back   Volume slider

Play/Pause   Progress bar

Figure 6-16: A movie with playback controls on Kindle Fire.

When you display a video's details in the Amazon Video Store, you can tap the Rental & Purchase Details link to view the terms of use for playing the video.

Playing Music

The ability to tap into Amazon's tremendous Music Store and sideload music from other sources by using a micro-B cable means that you can build up your ideal Music library and take it with you wherever you go.

Exploring the Music library

All your music is stored in the Music library (see Figure 6-17), which you display by tapping the Music button on the Kindle Fire Home screen. The currently playing or last played song and playback controls are located at the bottom of the screen.

The library is organized by Playlists, Artists, Albums, and Songs. Tap on any of these tabs to display the associated content.

At the bottom of the screen, in the Options bar, is a Back arrow to move you back one screen in the library, the Menu icon, and a Search icon to help you find pieces of music.

If you tap the Menu button, you see four additional options:

- ✔ **Downloads:** Tap Downloads to see items in the process of downloading, as well as completed downloads.
- ✔ **Settings:** Tap Settings to see options for entering an Amazon claim code, clearing the cache, enabling equalizer mode, and more.

Currently playing selection

Figure 6-17: The Music library is your central music repository.

- ✔ **Clear Queue or Now Playing:** This setting will change depending on whether you're displaying the currently playing music. From the list of songs in an album, tap Now Playing to display the currently playing music full screen with music playback controls (see Figure 6-18). If you are displaying the full screen of the currently playing music, tap the Clear Queue command to stop the music and go back to the Music library home screen.

- ✔ **Help:** Tap Help to get more information about using the Music app.

When you tap the Search button on the Options bar, you bring up a search field. Tap in the field and enter the title of a piece of music or a performer, and then tap Search on the onscreen keyboard. Kindle Fire displays results on each of the tabs in the Music library that match the search term(s).

Figure 6-18: Currently playing music.

Uploading music to the Cloud

One way to add music to your Kindle Fire Music library is by buying it from the Amazon Music Store.

You can also transfer a musical selection or collection stored on your computer (the music you've bought through iTunes, for example) by using a micro-B cable connection. (Read more about this process in Chapter 2.)

In addition, the Amazon Cloud allows you to upload music from your computer; after you upload music, it's available to you through your Kindle Fire Music library.

Follow these steps to upload music to the Amazon Cloud:

1. **Go to www.amazon.com/cloudplayer on your PC or Mac.**

2. **Sign into your Amazon account.**

3. **Tap the Upload Your Music button.**

   A dialog box appears, asking you to get the Amazon MP3 Uploader.

4. **Tap Download Now and follow the instructions that appear to install the Uploader.**

   After the Uploader has been installed, you see the Upload Music to Your Cloud Library dialog box.

5. **Tap the plus sign (+) to expand your musical selections on your computer and choose individual items.**

   Alternatively, don't choose anything at this point to upload all music from your computer to the Amazon Cloud.

6. **Tap the Start Upload button.**

   The dialog box shows the upload progress and lists the remaining items to be uploaded. Note that there's also an estimated time to upload the content shown in the dialog box.

After you upload items to your Amazon Cloud library, they are available to Kindle Fire on the Cloud tab of the Music library.

Opening and playing a song

To play music, you locate an item to play, and then you can use the playback toolbar to control the playback. Follow these steps to play music from your Music library:

1. **Tap the Music button on the Kindle Fire Home screen.**

2. **Locate an item you want to play on a tab in the Music library, such as Songs or Artists.**

3. **If you open a tab other than Songs, you need to tap to open an album or playlist to view the contents.**

4. **Tap to play it.**

   If you tap the first song in a group of music selections, such as an album or playlist, Kindle Fire begins to play all selections, starting with the one you tapped.

5. **Use the controls shown in Figure 6-19 to control playback.**

Tap the button with horizontal lines in the top-right of the screen to go back to the album or playlist the song belongs to. To go back to the Now Playing screen for the song, tap its image at the top-right of the screen.

Back | Forward
Shuffle Pause/Play Restart

Figure 6-19: Most of these tools are standard playback tools you've probably seen before.

Chapter 7

Ten Apps That Add Functionality

*K*indle Fire has functionality built in for consuming books, periodicals, music, and video, as well as a contact management app, web browser, and e-mail client. And, by adding apps to the device, you can easily acquire those tools you use regularly but that don't happen to be built into the Kindle Fire.

The Amazon Appstore, which you can learn to use in Chapter 4, contains thousands of cool apps for you to explore. To help you flesh out the basic tools in Kindle Fire, in this chapter I provide reviews of apps such as a calendar, note taker, and unit converter that meet your day-to-day needs and whet your *appe-tite*. Most of these are free.

From a nutrition guide to a very cool calculator app, these will provide fun and functionality for your Kindle Fire and not cost you much more than the time to download them.

SketchBook Mobile Express

From: AutoDesk, Inc.

Price: Free

SketchBook (see Figure 7-1) is a drawing app to satisfy the creative artist in your soul. With 47 preset brushes, you can draw whatever you can imagine on your Kindle Fire screen. You can control the brush characteristics and make use of an extensive color palette.

Figure 7-1: Sketchbook brings out the artist in you.

Try sideloading photos and modifying them with this clever app, then save your files in JPEG, PNG, or PSD formats. When you're done, it's easy to e-mail your artistic efforts to yourself to print from your computer.

The Brush Properties circular control lets you easily adjust the size and opacity of the writing tools. Touch the square at the top of the screen to access color controls and watch the Red, Blue, and Green levels adjust as you move around the color wheel.

Fast Food Nutrition Lite

From: FastFood.com

Price: Free

If you're watching your weight but are forced to scarf down fast food now and then, this little app could have an impact on your waistline. Not limited to traditional drive-thru fast food joints, the app gives you nutritional information about dishes from 100 restaurant chains, such as Applebees, Chili's, and Checker's, and includes over 25,000 menu items (see Figure 7-2).

Fast Food Nutrition Lite helps you keep track of calories, Weight Watchers points, fats, trans fats, saturated fats, cholesterol, sodium, carbohydrates, sugars, and protein. The calorie counter shows you how much of the recommended daily allowance each meal is providing you. Select the items you want in your meal and touch View Order, which displays a handy screen showing you all the totals for your meal.

You can add thumbnails for your favorite restaurants so that you don't have to search through all the restaurants to find the ones you like best.

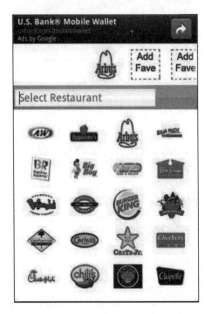

Figure 7-2: Track your calories with this handy counter.

aCalendar

From: Mathias Laabs

Price: Free

Kindle Fire has no built-in calendar app, so this one is a natural to add to your apps collection. This easy-to-use calendar app can help keep you on schedule (see Figure 7-3). You can display day, week, month, and birthday views. For you astronomers out there, you can even check the phases of the moon. The month screen displays black dots for full moons and a half-filled dot to indicate a half moon.

aCalendar makes great use of touchscreen gestures to let you easily move among views and take a look at event details. Swipe the screen horizontally to change among day, week, and month views. Swipe vertically to move from day to day, week to week, or month to month.

You can also add events to your calendar by simply pressing a date and filling in the name and time of your event.

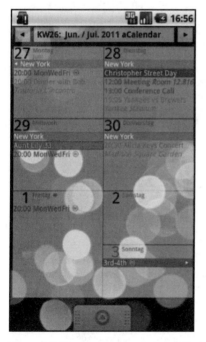

Figure 7-3: Keep track of your week with aCalendar.

Astral Budget

From: Astral Web, Inc.

Price: Free

Astral Budget helps you keep track of all your expenses, whether for a single trip or your yearly household budget. You can use built-in categories for fixed spending such as rent, food, travel, utilities, and so on to categorize your expenses.

The app has four sections: Goals, Expenses, Reports, and Export. Using these, you can enter the amounts you want to spend and track them against actual expenditures. You can use the wide variety of Reports in Astral Budget (see Figure 7-4) to examine your spending trends and even export data to your computer to examine with the more-robust application Excel. I like the Chart selections, including bar charts, pie charts, and list charts.

ColorNote Notepad Notes

From: Social & Mobile, Inc.

Price: Free

If being able to keep a to-do list warms the cockles of your organized (or disorganized) heart, this note-taking app is free and very simple to use.

You can keep a simple to-do list or other random notes, and even share information with your friends via e-mail, social networks, or messaging.

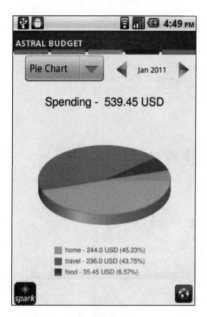

Figure 7-4: Use handy charts to visualize your spending practices.

ColorNote allows some nice word-processing-like functions, such as the capability to edit and cross items off lists that are completed (see Figure 7-5).

You can even set up reminders for items in your notes and search for specific content.

> If your notes are top secret, consider using the password feature in ColorNote.

Figure 7-5: When you finish an item on your list, check it off.

Cube Calculator

From: IP

Price: Free

This is a calculator with tons of bells and whistles, from the ability to use mathematical expressions and time calculations to logarithmic and trigonometric functions. There's a secondary keyboard for additional functions, such as cosines (see Figure 7-6).

Even if you're not a power math user, the very nice interface in this app makes casual calculations simple to do. Also, the help system for this app is actually helpful.

You can choose a theme such as Light or Dark to ease your eyestrain as you calculate. You can also control the maximum number of digits to be returned in a result.

Figure 7-6: The secondary keyboard offers even more functions.

Handrite Note

From: Ben Lee

Price: $2.99

If you miss the feeling of writing notes by hand, instead of typing them on plastic keyboards, this app is for you. It's simple to use: Tap to create a new note, and then use the spiral-bound pad interface to write words or draw images on the page with your finger. You can change the stroke width and text size for your writing and even use different colors (see Figure 7-7).

When you close the app, your note is saved, but you can press and hold the touchscreen to edit the text you entered. You can also create a label for a note and export it. The app isn't fancy; it's more for jotting down a phone number when you see a flyer about a missing kitten or making a quick note to yourself about what to pick up at the store. But for what it is, it's darn handy and easy to use.

Exchange by TouchDown

From: NitroDesk, Inc.

Price: Free

If you want to access e-mail, contacts, and calendar information from your workplace and your company uses Microsoft Exchange Server for these accounts, this little app will help you tap into your company e-mail. It touts itself as providing great security and provides the very handy service of wiping data from your Kindle Fire remotely if it's lost or stolen.

Figure 7-7: Writing on your Kindle Fire screen is very freeing.

Keep in mind that TouchDown doesn't work with IMAP or POP3 servers; it's intended for Exchange Servers, as well as supporting Zimbra, Kerio, and ActiveSync. Although the app has pretty-easy-to-use settings (see Figure 7-8), you might want to sit down over a cup of coffee with your network administrator to get this one working.

Figure 7-8: Make settings yourself or enlist the aid of your administrator.

Units

From: staticfree.info

Price: Free

If, like me, you need help converting just about any-thing to anything else (feet to meters, pounds to kilos, or whatever), you'll appreciate this handy little app. It handles 2,400 different conversions, including height, weight, volume, volume to weight, and time to distance. Tap the Unit key, and you'll see a list of the various types of conversions available (see Figure 7-9).

Just fill in the You Have field and the You Want field, and then enter the number of units. Tap the equal sign (=) and get your conversion. Holding Kindle Fire in landscape orientation displays a few more helpful tools on the calculator style interface.

Figure 7-9: Tap the Unit key to get a list of common units.

Wi-Fi Analyzer

From: farproc

Price: Free

Because Kindle Fire can connect to the web only through Wi-Fi, this handy app is helpful for keeping track of local Wi-Fi connections. You can observe available Wi-Fi channels and the signal strength on each (see Figure 7-10). There are several styles of graphs to choose from, including Channel, Time, Channel Rating, and Signal Meter.

Figure 7-10: Figure out whether your nearest Wi-Fi will help you connect.